Female Baggage

Understanding the Issues That Some Women Can Bring Into Relationships

Copyright

TABLE OF CONTENTS

INTRODUCTION

This is a book that will address what I call, "*Female Baggage*". The term Female Baggage is an expression that correlates with many varied but similar concepts within our society. Its general concern is with unresolved issues of an emotional nature. This emotional, psychological, or behavioral baggage can often be detrimental to a relationship. Each piece of baggage is created as a metaphorical image; it is that of carrying all the disappointments, wrongs and trauma of the past around with you, thus creating a heavy load on the mind, body, and spirit.

Baggage comes into play in a number of forms within relationships. These bags depict a given phenomenon or an idea that pervades many relationships today. Only the female baggage is covered in this book. There is a companion book titled: Male Baggage; Understanding The Burdens And Impediments That Men Bring Into Relationships, which covers the male aspect.

The following are covered in this book:
The Sleeping Bag, The Travel Bag, The Tea Bag, The Camera Bag, The Designer Bag, The Doggie Bag, and The Garbage Bag. There are also possible solutions for the problems discussed.

These terms which are often seen in a negative aspect, are created through life experiences. They may also be considered the recurrent bringing-up of the past from previous relationships. This may result in problems within the present relationship, and the individual becoming overloaded with negative energies that are unresolved from earlier times.

1

SLEEPING BAG

The Sleeping bag doesn't care about such issues, as commitment or love. Starting a family is a true absurdity for her. The only asset she recognizes as having value is her body. She believes in using what she has to gain what she wants. She is the archetypal female Casanova, a nymphomaniac by trade, pattern of behavior and choice. The Sleeping Bag is independent, she believes in the "trade", and feels that the answers to life questions, lies solely between her legs. This female masters the art of selection. She can be described as a bold sweet talker. Education and level of exposure does not "bag" The Sleeping Bag when it comes to men. She practices and perfects her art irrespective of time or place. There are no ceilings and no limits to how much pleasure she could give in order to have her way. For The Sleeping Bag, a man is merely a means to an end. The Sleeping Bag is fluid and witty, she is never dogmatic. She changes with the times and the seasons. She refines her art as time passes. Morality does not function in The Sleeping Bag's reality. Her body, she believes is the source of infinite power and prestige. She feels like a conqueror each time she has sex with a man. That man she has conquered and crossed on her tally; therefore, she has to move on, conquer more, and achieve more. History is replete with such women both in high places and a lot more who never got to enter into history books, but they made their mark in the sands of time and in the consciousness of many. History holds accounts of Cleopatra and her affairs with Caesar, and how much power and goodwill she was able to garner by the mere powers of seduction and being The Sleeping Bag to one of the greatest men in history at the time. Women over time have recognized this form of weakness, in the opposite sex and they have used it as a means to siphon all that they desire. Sometimes, the whore leaves a man broken and useless. The outcome of the short steamy relationship for The Sleeping Bag is always to win. To get what she wants; it doesn't matter to her if it is a win-win or a win-lose. She has evolved her strategy over time and is out to conquer the unassuming and the unguarded man, by fully exploiting her sexual powers.

She deploys everything in her arsenal. Lies or deception are tools and means to get past her mark. She moves to her mark with an air of decency to break free from the Madonna-whore complex. However, once she gets you to lower your defenses, she finds a way to get under your skin. She supplies you with pain and pleasure, satisfying your primal urges she makes the moment seem like eternity. She is the mistress of pleasure giving, she holds nothing back. She goes all out to satisfy, she fills your conscious momentarily until she's had enough of you then she will be gone with the wind. If you are in for the thrills, then you must watch out, so you aren't caught unaware. A Sleeping Bag enjoys the dynamics and uncertainty of her craft. Do not be deceived into thinking that you can tie her down. You don't have all that she needs. She wants the erratic, she wants the thrills and the danger of uncertainty appeals to her. All of these are not unitary qualities. Sex is her thing and she delights in the variety. Use extreme caution with The Sleeping Bag, lest she become your drug and addition. She will creep into or heart through the gates of pleasure, and once she is done with you, she will leave a void that cannot be filled by anyone else. The Sleeping Bag is infectious and poisonous. She has a hoard of men on her list based on her sexual needs. She will lead you down a slippery path and leave you hanging; your relationships, family and obligations are no concern of hers. The Sleeping Bag always has her emotions bagged up and shut tight. She jumps from one man to the other never revealing too much about herself. She shines her sparkling teeth and dreamy eyes, for the one thing that is her goal: Sexual Gratification.

According to a recently published paper written by Ari Armstrong, "...None of these girls was coerced into selling her body for money. Most of them come from middle-class backgrounds, and many had been accepted to universities. But they dropped out as soon as they realized they could make $20-30k a month as an escort..."

The Sleeping Bag cares less about intimacy and romance. These women do not care if they are seen with you or not, they want what they want. When she gets what she desires, she's out at the first opportunity. The big question for her is, "What's in it for me?" The term *Sleeping Bag* should not be confused as a dysfunction or a weakness. Rather it is their source of strength and self worth. According to research, there is no psychosocial difference between the sleeping bag and her other female counterpart. The difference might be in morals or from a mirrored viewpoint. According to a research in the Netherlands by Ine Vanwesenbeeck PhD, Manager of research at the Rutgers Nisso Group, Dutch Expert Center on Sexuality; "...female indoor sex workers in the Netherlands do not exhibit a higher level of work-related emotional exhaustion or a lower level of work related personal competence than a comparison group of female health care workers. The comparison group comprised of mostly nurses" The Sleeping Bag is not the worst of all creatures neither is she the laziest of all women. She puts a lot of effort into her craft. She is bold and fearless, wise and cunning like the female courtiers in the ancient courts. She knows how to keep a king, the high and mighty of society wrapped around her fingers; they are at her beck and call. She doesn't flock, she is not your regular hoe in the red light districts. She is wise and strong like the eagle, she chooses and swoops down on her pray ferociously and then devours. At other times she creeps in like a worm, she devours slowly and in the end, she leaves a carcass filed with emptiness. She could be the product of a dysfunctional home, or from a home dominated by an Alpha female. To her, men are but things or marks to conquer. The Sleeping Bag fears domination and restriction, hence her phobia of commitment. They consider commitment only when it becomes the last resort and when it provides an opportunity for further adventure. The Sleeping Bag explores her feminine powers to the fullest, she understands men on a greater level than most men understand themselves. From her perspective, she is the ultimate woman. Patrick Rothfuss wrote in his book, *In the name of the Wind* "Call a jack a jack. Call a spade a spade.

But always call a whore a lady." This whore is the lady who explores femininity without physical, emotional or psychological restrictions.

The freedom to sleep around is not the only goal for her. It might sound hilarious but some Sleeping Bags have come to justify themselves by having a kind of Deus ex machina view of themselves. Some say they help to save marriages. They claim that if a woman cannot adequately satisfy her man, then they are there to do the "dirty job", without having a psychological or emotional attachment. The service they render comes at a price, a negative, and a positive price as viewed from the reference frame of the observer and the performer. The extreme form of The Sleeping Bag, are the prostitutes in the red light district and street corners. These women are lower in the food chain. Their decision making abilities are limited due to most of them being hooked on drugs and others being under the control of pimps. The archetypal Sleeping Bag is an independent woman, who takes pride in what she does. She has complete control over her space and time. The Sleeping Bag will not call herself a prostitute. She defines the game in which she plays, she sets the rules. For her, the rules are never constant; they change with the players and the time. The Sleeping Bag masters the use of smoke screens and other deception props. When you are tangled up with her, it is either that you are sincerely ignorant of her play, or you just want to enjoy the thrills that come with the trip down the spiral of uncertainty. The Sleeping Bag is not the same person to everyone. It is not to say that she has a multiple personality disorder. It is a craft that she masters. She knows that needs vary from person to person, and she knows that she has to use a multifaceted approach to meet the needs of those she comes across. One might be prompted by naivety to ask what causes or what elicits the behavior? The simple answer is that there are as many different and unique reasons as there are Sleeping Bags. Some get hooked by the financial aspect, some by the power, some the fun and pleasure and yet others may be motivated by the risk and danger involved in the art they have meticulously crafted.

The Sleeping Bag is everywhere, not just in the pubs and bars, she is the secretary. She is the boss and the colleague. She is the police officer who has sized up men on both sides of the law. She is the attendant in the store and the waitress in a restaurant. She is the woman next door; she is the baby sitter and the house cleaner. She is the strict teacher and the adorable whore. She has her web spread far and wide waiting patiently for her unassuming prey. If you realize you have been caught in the web of The Sleeping Bag, you would want to get away, but the more you struggle to break free, the more entangled you become, the secret is to remain still. It is said…"You cannot see your reflection in flowing waters."

Just be still while you calculate your exist strategy, and while you do, hope that she leaves you the way she met you. When The Sleeping Bag becomes your "addiction" then you are at her mercy. This is because she is your drug, your addiction and your dealer. The sleeping bag leaves a trail of broken hearts and sometimes broken homes in her travels. She cares nothing about your emotions and your addiction. When she's done with you she has to move on. For The Sleeping Bag, the only consequences to fear are those that come from stagnation and commitment. She is not your bitch, even though she might want you to believe that she is, but then, she is the bitch. The word "promiscuous" is used to describe The Sleeping Bag. Promiscuity means "having short term sexual relationship with many partners, without really engaging in an exclusive relationship with these partners" this is from a paper by Markey, P.M and Markey C.N. in 2007 titled "The interpersonal meaning of sexual promiscuity" in the formal of research in personality. The initial inspiration could be similar for Sleeping Bags, but for each individual it is very unique.

2

THE TRAVEL BAG

This is the type of woman that never settles down. Marriage and commitment are not her thing. Neither ranks high on her scale of importance. She is the ace career woman who puts her career ahead of every other thing, including herself. The Travel Bag is always on the move. She is moving against the tides of reality. She is the woman who sees relationship as a fool's gambit. She sees husbands and children as anchors and babies as things. She never settles down and is rationally confused. In what she assumes to be self-centeredness, she is not even the center of focus. Her career or whatever she engages in becomes her drug and addiction. The Travel Bag is a disaster waiting to happen in the fullness of time. The Travel Bag proclaims the creed of independence. Interdependence is claimed only when her career is the focal point. A relationship with her has a short temporal scale. The Travel Bag is the lone wolf, she bosses, and lords over others or she keeps to herself while she pushes up the ladder of her career. She is the rising star, the person to watch out for, she is the first female this and the first female that; she is the only female in board meetings and she carries her surname for the greater part of her life. The Travel Bag never has enough time for friends or family, and she is quick to give excuses for being late or absent. The Travel Bag may become extremely nice at some point. There are times when she might bear gifts and exhibit unusual friendliness. Don't be surprised when this happens, and don't be fooled into thinking that she has changed. The only reason she will do this is to solve an immediate problem or quarrel. It is never as a result of change. When they fall in love, it is with themselves and their careers. The man or woman who craves their attention loses a thousand times. They could have short sexual relationships with bosses and people above them in rank who are key components to their career advancement. It is not news that female actors sleep with directors just to get movie roles. This tendency is not unique to the movie industry; it is everywhere, from white-collar jobs to blue-collar jobs. Sometimes, The Travel Bag can be said to have a mild form of Narcissistic Personality Disorder (NPD). This can simply be described as a disorder in which a person becomes pre-occupied excessively, with personal gains, prestige, achievement, or power. The narcissistic Travel Bag has an over inflated sense of importance or what could be called a "bloated" self-esteem. They feel like the world revolves around them "When you are involved with a Travel Bag, she always points out what makes you small, or why you are not good enough. Trying to satisfy a Travel Bag is like trying to fill up a basket with water. She is nagging bitch, the perfectionist who never gets satisfied.

If you ever manage to find yourself in relationship with a Travel Bag, you must have been lucky enough to shoot yourself in the foot. This woman will keep you on the edge. She will do all that she can to turn the table around and to become the dominant partner in the relationship. She will not stop until she's had enough, however she is never satisfied. One important thing to know about The Travel Bag is that her loyalty is never fixed. Honor is but a word like any other whose meaning will fade into the background of priority. She masters the art of funning when it is in the favor of her career to act accordingly. This woman's loyalty is determined by personal advancement goals. She is loyal when the wind blows in her favor and when things go south for her, relationships and friendships do as well. The Travel Bag is all too busy to live the life that eludes her, her priorities are skewed. She does not care about life issues, and truly doesn't care about the next person. There are signs to watch out for that may be subtle indicators of this kind of personality. Watch out for simple words like "me" or "I" in her conversation. When these words dominate the conversation, you should raise your guard. You must learn more about her priorities and her life philosophy before you are trapped in her miry web of bitterness. The Travel Bag in most cases is smart and intelligent. Her looks are not important, but the more attractive she is the higher the wall of arrogant pride around her.

The Travel Bag is overly loyal when she stands before her superiors as well as her inferiors, yet only when she needs them in order to move on or to achieve certain goals. The Travel Bag is not the most loved or appreciated person. She only keeps people close with a tight leash. People fear, but do not respect her. She has a great lack of empathy and respect for others. If you are around The Travel Bag, you want to make yourself highly invaluable, even as a subordinate, that way you will get to keep your head above her poisonous waters. This type of woman is not a moralist, neither is she overly religious. When she is, it is only at face value. She lives by her own "logical" standards, by her own rules. The Travel bag does not flock, her way of life does not call for group thinking. She may have a handful of friends about her; these friends will only save to reinforce her way of thinking and behavior. This female is not hard to pick out of a crowd, her words and her demeanor will all betray her, as she walks around with sky-high shoulders, her dry and stern voice barking out commands. She is excessively prideful, always annoyed and angered by the inconsequential, continuously making mountains out of molehills. According to psychologists "Hubris is the emotion elicited when success with regards to one's standards, rules and goals, is applied to a person's entire self. People inclined to be hubristic evaluate their actions positively and then say to themselves: 'I have succeeded. I am a success.' Often, hubris is considered an undesirable trait to be avoided." The Travel Bag's behavior is reinforced by success; it could be an innate or a learned tendency. People who are prone to this arrogant pride will always want to relive the high that it comes with. They will seek to recreate scenarios that bring about such feelings. This is the reason why they always act bitchy. For The Travel Bag it is both an addiction and a way of life, nothing else matters, but the way she feels. To achieve this constant high, according to Morrison (1989), The Travel Bag might alter her standards, her goals, or rules so that she can re-evaluate the meaning of success from a perspective in which she is comfortable. The hubristic Travel Bag does not separate herself from the success that drives her crazy. To her, the object, and the subject are the same. Pride is beautiful and an awesome source of motivation for higher achievements, but as the saying goes "pride goes before a downfall." For The Travel Bag reality dawns on her along the pathways of time. She rejects these thoughts, up until she realizes that she is running out of time. In actual reality she is "the bitch", but when the reality of it finally dawns upon her, she tries make up for lost time. If you are unfortunate, you might just fall for her deceitful charms. Once you have her under your wings she becomes the worm of your destruction. She is a woman who has perfected the art of manipulation. If you are not yourself a player, then, you might want to take a bow and get out. Otherwise this Delilah might just cut off your hair. She will take away your pride and all that makes up your personality. Hubris, which is one of the dominant emotional states of The Travel Bag is hard to understand and harder yet, to study. When dealing with a Travel Bag, you must look out for the early warning signs. You must prepare your mind for the next line of action; the consequences be damned, or assume a defensive position. You may try hard to alter The Travel Bag's point of view about the reality of things, but you must be careful how much of yourself you invest in the quest. The Travel Bag is ruthless she sees through people, she picks her victims with great care, and she capitalizes on their weakness. If you ever get caught-up with her, keep your secrets and your weaknesses as far away from her as possible. She is never a team player. She is only on your team as directed by the course of events. She plays games with your head, your thoughts, and your emotions. Once she has control over the situation, you become her puppet; she pulls all the strings. She will challenge herself to do nasty things just for the high she gets from her actions. "Some people try to be tall by cutting off the heads of others." Paramahansa-Yogananda. When you are caught up with the dominant Travel Bag, be sure to keep your head low and give her the illusion of greatness.

This is a unique survival strategy. According to Doctor Dario Maestripieri, in a paper entitled Social Dominance Explained, he said; "Behaving submissively to the dominant is advantageous to the subordinate only as a short-term strategy, to give the subordinate some time to acquire physical strength or political power to mount an effective rebellion against the dominant." This is a true and sure strategy for working against The Travel Bag, using her own venom against her. She wants to be the ultimate solution, so she creates tailor made problems. She is like the Allelopallic plant that suppresses the growth of other plants around her. She wants you to remain in the inferior position; she wants no challenge for her exalted position.

According to an article in The Social Pathologist in 2009, "...the alpha dominant female is the person who calls the shots in a relationship. She dictates the terms. When challenged, she will not defend but attack. Insulted, she knows no limit in reply. Slighted she will seek her vengeance. If the relationship is not to her liking, she walks. What we have in such an individual is akin to Nietzsche's "will to power". These women have incredible psychological strength. This is the type of woman that is able to triumph against adversity alone. They are incredibly successful in nearly everything they undertake... except their personal lives." The only Alpha female that is happy, is the one that has found a man that is more assertive than she is. This woman is known as the Alpha submissive, the Alpha dominant travels alone. If you are aware that you cannot take the heat generated from this female, get out of her kitchen or simply do not go in at all.

3

THE TEA BAG

This is the type of woman that thinks that she is God's gift to men. She has a bad attitude and she thinks she is the finest thing walking the face of the earth. She is stuck up and really into her looks, she is what a man will call STANK.

The Tea Bag is that woman who has a compulsive narcissistic tendency; she wants to be the center of attention, being beautiful is her compulsion. She has a mild form of obsessive-compulsive disorder. She is the skin and the beauty expert; she could spend a fortune on beauty products. She looks at men as mirrors through which she sees herself. She is the object of her own infatuation. She understands the weather and the seasons only as it applies to her beauty and looks.

The Tea Bag is the most of all women; she is never completely in love with another. The Tea Bag is never the soloist. She remains in the company of people who reinforce her narcissistic behaviors. She walks among those who give compliments and who supply beauty products and or advice. She surrounds herself with admirers and always seeks attention. She walks in the shoes of geocentricism. She does not commit to anyone without sufficient benefits; she is too good-looking to be one person's business. She feels fragile and beautiful like the butterfly, she is lazy and would not get her hands dirty for any reason, unless it applies to her beauty and looks.

This narcissist looks at herself as the axis upon which the earth rotates; she walks in her own projected glass slippers. She is choosy, in what she eats; whom she moves with and in everything that surrounds her person. She practices the doctrine of "Me" 'Myself" and "I", she comes first. – Always.

According to Dr. Samuel Lopez De Victoria, "at the core of extreme narcissism is the egotistical preoccupation with self, personal preferences, aspiration, needs, success, and how he/she is perceived by others." Some amount of narcissism is healthy, but The Tea Bag takes it far to the extreme. She can become overly annoying with her tendencies of self-absorption. She lacks empathy and is very prone to jealousy, especially when the spotlight is not on her. She always has a handful of harsh remarks and criticisms. She always passes derogatory comment towards her peers, when the subject of discussion is beauty.

The Tea Bag is capable of being loyal and submissive, only when you are the source of reinforcement for her drive toward being the best when it comes to the issue of beauty. Give her a box of cosmetics and she's your bitch. Shower her with praises as it regards to her beauty, and she will always come back to you for more. If her strive for perfection does not concern you, then you are parallels. The obsession of The Tea Bag with herself could be attributed to a thousand and one reasons. Being overly self indulgent, to her is not a bad thing and in all truth, she doesn't even recognize it. From her point of view, she only takes good care of herself and looks out for her appearance. The Tea Bag is a shopaholic who will always want to keep up with the fashion that is trending at that moment; sometimes, she is the hard worker who works only for the sake of her appearance. Her priorities are always skewed. She is prone to misunderstandings. This is because what to her is seen as innocent pomposity is nothing but mere arrogance to others.

Look out for The Tea Bag, she always surrounds herself with people that are less attractive than herself, if she is a 6 she surrounds herself with people who are less attractive, maybe 4's or 3's, she consciously does this to highlight herself as the center of attraction. She always wants to be the bulls-eye, and she always has a way of craftily achieving that. If you are her man, she will find a way to compel you to step up, or she will relegate you into the background if you refuse to match her prowess.

The Tea Bag's loyalty does not go above her beauty. She will not tolerate anything that comes between her and her beauty, although the object and the subject are one and the same in this case. The Tea Bag will do anything for her looks; she is not really a fan of childbearing, because she cannot stand the "ugly" look for nine months; she will do any and everything to preserve her beauty. If you are caught up with The Tea Bag, you might want to turn up the heat and be more assertive, or just give her clearly defined options.

The Tea Bag views life from the mirrored perspective of "beautiful" or "ugly", everything to her has to be on one side of the spectrum, directly or indirectly representing a side. Satisfaction and worth are measured along the lines of beauty. The Tea Bag is proud, but not hubristic like The Travel Bag. She can be a loving person, when she wants to, but this state is only sustained as long as it is reinforced by factors, which bring about satisfaction to her.

It is true that beauty is in the eyes of the beholder, but for this female, "she is" the standard of beauty and every element of beauty revolves around her. She is not necessarily the most stunning creature, but she has an over rated view of herself. Whoever shares this view with her becomes her friend, and whoever doesn't, is her foe. She is intimidating and unapproachable as a result of the standards she sets for herself. The Tea Bag has mastered the art of cosmetology she is her own laboratory. The Tea Bag often builds a wall around her insecurities, she feels beautiful, she wants to be noticed, but she doesn't truly have a great self-esteem. As Dr. Dale Archer puts it, "Low self-esteem is more common in beautiful women, than you would expect.

Some just don't believe they are attractive. They have a distorted self image and don't believe others who tell them how stunning they are. Thus in their mind everyone is a 'liar' and not to be trusted." The Tea Bag in most cases is not the worst of people, but sometimes she lives in the illusion, which tends to make her a terrible bore. She is at most times not satisfied with the way she looks, and is always looking for newer and more innovative ways to get more our of her physical appearance. The Tea Bag is easy to tame and to get under control, but first you must understand the underlying factors for her behavior.

There could be any number of reasons for her actions, once you have them figured out, you can go to work on putting her in check. This doesn't mean a total reversal in attitude, but it could be "putting a box around her." Taming her and letting her have her thing within the circle of reason.

However, if you are her man, you must be assertive. Assertiveness is sexy to women who are not homosexual, they always like a strong man for protection and support.

Psychologists have come up with the notion of the multifaceted nature of self, with different parts that help make up the synergistic whole; these parts include self-esteem, self-perception, self-knowledge, and self-awareness. All these aspects of a person's personage are key to the overall functioning of the social identity. The Tea Bag tends to exaggerate the aspect of self-awareness and self-perception, while relegating the other aspects to the background and sometimes relegated to oblivion.

The Tea Bag is sometimes like an annoying child who wants to show off her new toys or dress, and sometimes she misses the timing, and simply becomes a nuisance. Only in the case of The Tea Bag, she is the object that she wishes to show off. According to Kohut in the book How does Analysis Cure "Self objects are objects which we experience as part of our self; the expected control over them is, therefore, closer to the concept of control which a grownup expects to have over his own body and mind, than to the concept of control which he expects to have over others."

The Tea Bag is not pathological, she's just a little messed up in the head, but that can be straightened out, with a change of perception and a general shift in her outlook towards life. The Tea Bag could be infectious, but she can be lived with. Like the saying goes, if you can't join her, beat her.

4

THE CAMERA BAG

As the name implies this is the woman who tries to take a glimpse of things that don't concern her, she is sneaky and always pry's into her man's business. She is the spy who delights in tormenting her man with suspicion. She wants to know what he is doing, who he has been with, and every damn thing about anything that doesn't concern her.

The Camera Bag is insecure and in most cases, she has a low self esteem. She rides on the waves of her insecurities and she becomes a nuisance for all who are around her. The insecurities and other manifest behaviors of The Camera Bag are not attributed to a deficit in education. The manifest behaviors of The Camera Bag may be a result of some defect in her upbringing. One of or both her parents could be cheaters, or she could have grown up in a broken home. The Camera Bag can be very submissive in the onset of a relationship, but somewhere along the line she would want to put her scent on everything in order to mark her territory. The Camera Bag lives on the edge. She wants to remain at the helm of affairs, and call the shots. This is the primary reason for her behavior. She does all the 'boring" stuff to remain relevant. Sometimes jealousy and illogical fears of the unknown elicit such behaviors.

One word that captures her habits is suspicion. She always thinks that you are cheating on her with just about anyone. She thinks there should be a plan and a routine for your life. Five minutes late or five minutes early would raise her suspicious if you wear a new cologne or change your hair style, she could go all the way in keeping tabs on you. The Camera Bag will always want things to be done in her favor, she is likened to a prosecuting attorney; she puts whoever is involved with her on the stand, and she asks the hard line questions. It must be pointed out at this point that the behavior of The Camera Bag might not be entirely uncalled for, sometimes when the situation calls for suspicion one has to act on it, but when it becomes a habit, and disproportionately shown there is a problem.

The Camera bag will always have a good explanation for all of her actions. She will make such statements as, "you know, you can't trust...", "they are always acting that way, so you just have to keep an eye on them." The Camera Bag can be a thorn in the flesh. Sometimes one gets to think that pass codes were created because of this spy. When she is involved with a person, especially her man, she will always go through his phone, wallet and email. She is the unpaid agent who works really hard to seek out the irrelevant. She acts based on gossips and hear say. She will take any kind of information and use it in order to address about her man.

Another funny reality about The Camera Bag is that she will in most cases, be protective of her man, but right in front of him, she is also the vicious critic and antagonist. The Camera Bag cuts across all character types the melancholy, the sanguine, the hot-tempered and the docile. She is everywhere. She is the nurse and the supervisor, the sales representative and the technician, and everything else in between. The thinking of The Camera Bag is to always stay ahead. She believes in her wit and in her ability to keep everything under control, and the best way she believes she can do that, is to keep tabs on everything and most especially, by spying on everything and everyone around her. Use caution in relationships with this type of woman. There is all possibility that she knows everything about you thanks to the spy that she is. She believes she can bring about perfection in a relationship through the acquisition of information.

The Camera Bag wants to know what you would think she doesn't know. Sometimes, she will approach you with a ready-made solution, and you get to think that she has a good ability to read the situation. The Camera Bag can be irrationally protective, she is like the king cobra, she will strike anything that possesses any threat to her way of thinking or her many insecurities. Get to know her, before you get involved with her. She never misses any opportunity to pry into your life at the initial stages it might come as subtle harmless advice, or questions. Raise your defense systems when she asks questions and start wondering how she got to know certain information. She doesn't seek to know for any plausible reason, she is sick and obsessed with the affairs of others. Stay away from her. She will rope you into the miry waters of confused self-indulgence. Her girlfriends are not even free from her whims, she wants to know how every bit of their lives are run. She wants to know how they get money for a new pair of shoes, nails, hair and fragrance. The Camera Bag does not stay within her boundaries, the best she can do is to hang on the fence and keep a steady watch on your affairs. When you confront her, she sees nothing wrong in her actions. She insists that she has done nothing wrong; she calls for proof and argues needlessly.

Unless you want to live in a world of constant scrutiny, transparency (in every sense of the word), or in the world of locks, pass codes, and crypts then you would do well to stay clear of The Camera Bag. She will always show up at your office and break all protocols, just to catch her man in the act of something. She feels she has every right to be wherever her man is, if he doesn't have anything to hide. When her man is having a night out with friends, she is somewhere lurking in the dark, with a camera or some other recording device. The basis behind this behavior is to allow her a reason to ask you hard line questions the next day, such as: "Who is that woman?", "Why is she all over you?" "Can you explain what was happening here?" Whenever you leave the house the questions are endless and her suspicions remain if there is anything she doesn't know about every moment.

She trains herself to become the ultimate hacker, to break passcodes and locks. The Camera Bag will have the contact information of all your friends and will want to become friends with them also. This is not out of mutual respect or any personal liking, but to keep "her man" in check. The Camera Bag may be obsessively in love, or a habitual heart breaker with trust issues. Sometimes your female friends and colleagues come under fire. They get calls and threats from the "owner" of the man or woman as the case may be. As stated earlier, the crux of her issues may be built around trust that is lacking. However, it could be a maniacal way to scandalously punish her man.

Sometimes she comes up with such gimmicks when she wants out of the relationship. All the effort she will religiously put into the search for evidence is to gain her passport out of the relationship. This could also be a defense mechanism for her. Maybe she has her hands in other cookies jars. Therefore, it becomes a race of whose cover gets blown first. When you notice The Camera Bag mounting too much pressure to catch you in the act, then it might be time to confront her. Sometimes it is best to stop and put her under the microscope, all the push and the pressure might only be a smoke screen to put the vial of sainthood over her shady dealings. Never trust her enough to believe that she is a victim in any circumstance. She is conscious of all of her activities and all the pressure that might be mounting is deliberate. It is an art of war for this woman with a

Machiavellian outlook on things. She is ruthless and always ready to undermine whoever or whatever stands in her way, by any means of black mail. Hence, the endless information she acquires. According to a paper titled "Suspicious Mind" published by Daniel Freeman in the Clinical Psychology Review of May 2007, Freeman said, "At least 10 – 15% of the general population regularly experience paranoid thoughts and persecutory delusions are a frequent symptom of psychosis....There is also evidence that anomalous internal experiences may be important in leading to odd thought content, and that a jumping into conclusion reasoning bias, is present in individuals with persecutory delusions."

5

THE DESIGNER BAG

Before we move further, let us look at the meaning of "The Designer Bag", and what she represents. The Designer Bag creates a world of her own. She lives in the clouds; far above the level of normalcy, only the glittery, the shiny, and the expensive appeal to her. She wants designer everything, clothes, handbags, shoes and accessories. She is the lover of high-end products. She is the seductress and the mistress. She walks with the finest in society, as a means to an end, or to live the synthetic life she has created for herself. The Designer Bag is not the most loyal of women. She is an addict of the high life. The Designer Bag will break a man if he lets her, and she is capable of using the last of all resources to buy the latest designer products.

The Designer Bag is the ultimate shopaholic, she just has to keep up with the trends and live up to her imaginary expectations. She is always in competition with herself and the likes of her. The Designer Bag cannot tell the difference between a "need" and a 'want". She is in a state of constant "high". Her condition ranges from a mild to chronic obsessive compulsive disorder. She lives in a state of constant compulsion in order to live up to expectation that coexists with the things that she treasures. She runs while no one is chasing. The Designer Bag is not just, about what she wears, when it comes to culinary practices, she chooses the finest restaurants with fancy menus. She doesn't believe in stressing to make meals for herself. There are good chefs and good restaurants to take care of all the busy work of cooking. She hangs around the biggest restaurants, even if it is for a glass of the cheapest wine, which affords her the opportunity of name-dropping. The Designer Bag is not necessarily the wealthiest or the most intelligent in society; neither is she the smartest. She is the copycat that wants to live up to standard; she wants to be like the celebrities on TV. She wants to act and live like the beautiful and cooked up characters in movies; these are her role models. She wants to be the center attraction in her reality, just like her role models in the movies. She has an illusion of overlapping realities. She hangs around expensive bars, gorgeously dressed;

waiting for the unfortunate man that will walk up to her and buy her a drink. She laughs out loud, even when there are no jokes, she wants to be noticed, and she wants to be reckoned with.

The Designer Bag only saves when there is a need or a compulsion to get a new product or service. She could go to the extreme of starving herself, or denying herself of basic life necessities just to get a temporary satisfaction.

The Designer Bag is always "name dropping" just to feel important or to create a false image in the mind of others. She attends celebrity parties and gathering just to get back up for her celebrity friends list claims. She will beg for autographs and selfies when amongst the social elite, and she will add these posts on her social media profiles. With the untrue evidence in place, she can go on to make huge claims, usually indirect and ambiguous, to keep her head, in case of any backfire. The Designer Bag comes in different forms and is created through varied circumstances. Sometimes she is from an affluent background and sometimes from a modest background. The type from the modest background is the most pretentious type. She is the most insecure. She is the ultimate miser, always calculating her finances. She will save a little only to burn it down on the irrelevant just to have a sense or feeling that she is among them or that she belongs.

The second type is from an affluent background. She was brought up with an ostentatious outlook on life; life for her is a bed of roses. In her way of thinking anyone in her life can either maintain the status quo, make things better or lose their relevance. She is pampered and spoiled. One terrible characteristic of The

Designer Bag is that she is so interested in spending but, has little to no interest in the wealth creation process. All that concerns The Designer Bag is need and glamour. She reads magazines about food, wine and fashion. She is always knowledgeable of the latest trends. She knows her automobiles only by their worth and the caliber of people who own them. The Designer Bag's main weakness is in her self-indulgence. Her obsessive compulsive disorder is backed up by a structure of narcissism, on the social media, and acting to open up channels of following. She wants to be celebrated. She is an admirer and lover of that which lies outside her reach. She is engaged in an eternal chase of flimsy glory. If you have any dealings with this type of woman, you don't want to trust her with your finances. Otherwise, you may wake up one day to find your life savings in vested in a piece of clothing. Do not trust her entirely with your health or wellbeing either, her physical appearance is the first thing on her mind. When a boil or acne appears on her face, she panics as if she was diagnosed with a malignant cancer. The Designer Bag has a skewed sense of reality. She takes uncalculated financial risks without a second thought. She will go on a diet on the first promise that it will solve some problems of her physical appearance.

The Designer Bag does not want to age and she is in constant search for the elixir of youth. She wants her skin to remain young and glowing, her breasts and hair to maintain their youthful appearance even when she is fifty and beyond. She can spend a fortune on all kinds of formulas and mixes to chase the illusion of eternal youth. Sometimes one could be compelled to think that she is acting out a fairytale, script-fantasies and illusions. The Designer Bag doesn't have any use for a man of lower ranking; she sees everything in the light of social status. This explains her need for up-scale items. A man of lower social ranking is to her like an everyday item such as a common no name brand pair of socks. This is something that just anyone can pick up, and thus she has diminished interest in such an item or person. It is true that birds of a feather flock together, if the male of lower social ranking shares her illusion of grandiosity there is a chance that he has a shot at getting her attention, even if she knows he has a humble background. The Designer Bag is a materialist, and she cares little about spirituality or morality, all she cares about is the physical. She revels in compliments; she tries hard to stand out in the social crowd. She could be an awesome lover, but her man has to be a lover of fashion, or the source and reinforcement of her beauty. Sometimes she works hard and plays hard, but in the general sense, she plays harder than she works. Her self-esteem is directly proportional to her social standing. In circles where she is not among the socially elite, she looks upon herself as lesser. The ways of The Designer Bag can be treacherous, however with little rewards. Sometimes she goes back to ground zero to start all over again as a result of terrible decisions. However, there are those rare times when she will meet up with luck and good fortune. The Designer Bag would do anything for her idols, in most cases she throws herself at the ones she admires, her fashion and glamour gods. When she has the opportunity to sleep with celebrities, she walks away feeding blessed. According to Elizabeth Harney, PhD, "The stereotype of the typical shopaholic is a cheerful, superficial, trendy young woman who is concerned with little more than the latest shoes and handbags, is a common image in our society." Harney further states that studies have shown that the shopaholic is of low self-esteem; thus she uses shopping and the endless accumulation of fashionable items to boost her esteem, or to create an illusion of a glorified self-image.

The Designer Bag is an archetypal representation of the modern woman who has lost herself in the continuously changing trends of fashion. The Designer Bag understands the chemistry of makeups and her skin, but not the chemistry of relationships or that of her man.

The Designer Bag rides on the waves of the unending compliments that come from her admirers and others who reinforce her behavior. When you come across a Designer Bag, she always wants you to notice her clothes and accessories, she wants to be seen. That is the essence of who she is. This woman tends to look down upon people who have no means of keeping up with the latest fashion trends.

The true nature of The Designer Bag is seen behind the scene, where no one is watching. That is when her true self is manifested. Behind all the glitter and glamour which gets projected into the view of many, might be a disgusting small woman

6

THE DOGGIE BAG

This ultimate drama queen cares less about what others think. She is all about herself, always in a state of constant excitement. She will heat up the polity for the fun of it. She is always excited by disquiet and noise. The drama woman is flashy and loud always meddling in other people's affairs and giving opinions even when they are not requested or needed. She just wants to assert herself. The Doggie Bag sees her man as a constant source of excitement. She drives him crazy at every opportunity and for every flimsy reason. The drama queen does not need a good reason to start a fight, she enjoys the disturbance, disquietude excites her. Her loyalty is not deeply rooted, much like that of many of the women discussed within these pages. This dramatic woman has some traits of The Camera Bag, she knows about all the shady things going on around her, if you want the latest information about anything or anyone; just engage her in conversation. The Doggie Bag is shameless and docsn't care about what people are saying about her or her attitude. For The Doggie Bag, everything is dispensable, even her man and her relationships. She has such an inflated sense of independence that nothing matters to her or is seen as important enough to make her "behave accordingly". The drama woman is the source of all gossips and petty talks, in a neighborhood. She can tell you who is sleeping with who and under what conditions. She will tell detailed tales of how the next woman lost or couldn't find a man, while she is in a dysfunctional relationship or does not have a man. The Doggie Bag has a scandalous hand in every kind of negative mess going on. She has a shallow sense of consequence. The drama woman has a confused sense of good and bad, and is very low on the emphatic scale. The Doggie Bag is in most cases, an uneducated or the half educated woman. Her friends are mostly people with her kind of mindset, these are the people that feed her the information she so proudly disseminates. She is like the powerhouses of small talks and gossips. The drama queen operates at a very low cognitive level and she sees nothing wrong with her view of the world, predominately because she doesn't have any other view of the world. An old Japanese proverb say "I no naka no kawazu, taikai wo shirazu." Translated it reads; "The toad in the well does not know about the great ocean." The drama woman feels like the center of gravity in her little world. She constantly stirs things up just to remain relevant. When there is no external opponent, she has to create drama. This drama queen will strike at her own children just to maintain the flow of excitement. Before you get involved with this type of woman you might want to weigh the pros and cons of taking her under your wings. There are subtle signs that would serve as indicators. At the early stages it might be difficult to discern, the kind of person you are dealing with, but watch out for garrulous nature. She may try so hard to conceal this, but it will always find a way of showing itself. Another thing to watch out for is the chain of little complaints and comparisons. She will inevitably pick on one person you both know, and she will dissect the affairs of that person to the state of a critical analysis. She is the unpaid commentator. She can chatter for hours on without end, saying things that are not backed by facts and sometimes not even by common sense. Although common sense is an attribute that is not common across the board, sometimes this woman acts jaw-droopingly foolish. She shouts at the top of her voice when she tries to drive home her point. She is an archetypal termagant. She nags the living hell out of her man and children. She is always dissatisfied with what everyone does, she wants things to always go her way. When they don't, all hell breaks lose. As she divulges the secrets of others to you, you can be very sure that your secrets with her are likened to water poured into a basket. Sometimes she may be kind enough to keep your secrets for a while, but they are sure to come out when things are no longer right between the two of you. The Doggie Bag is always a power wedge between her man and his family, and sooner or later, he might have to make the hard choice between keeping his family and chasing a flimsy illusion. The drama woman knows how to get under your skin. She comes to you with her tail between her legs then she opens up her secrets to you. Be careful here, her secrets mean nothing to her; they could be boldly written on the dollar bills or the Hollywood hills for all she cares. She earns your trust this way. The next step is to feed you some personal information about someone you might be interested in. You are now lured into the cycle of repayment. All she has done so far is to hand you her bargaining chip. She wants to have dirt on everyone, and once she gets what she wants, you will then realize that the loyalty she gave you was like frozen water, solid at the point when everything was cool, but you will quickly realize that you have nothing when things get heated up. Rest assured, they are absolutely going to get heated up. It is in her nature to shake things up a little. She cannot do without it.

7

GARBAGE BAG

This a woman that does not worry about anything, she is the non-affectionate. Everything goes for her and she doesn't care about what happens to her. Nor does she care about the consequences of her actions and inactions. The Garbage Bag seems not to care about anything. She is the type of woman that takes life as it comes, and in most cases, she doesn't believe that there is anything she can do to change the state of things. The Garbage Bag comes in two extremes, the lazy type, and the hard working type. The lazy Garbage Bag sits around and waits for things to sort themselves out. Her house is always littered and messy sometimes she is too lazy to even take care of herself. She is the nonchalant type she could toy with a man for his wealth and his emotions.

Everything is fun to her, when she is not the hardworking type. This woman has lost her affection as a result of what I will term "confused affections". The Garbage Bag as the name suggests, is the "Yes" woman. She agrees to the proposal of anyone who comes her way, and when he's done, he drops her and moves on. She remains heart broken only for a while, until the next person comes around. The cycle repeats itself and she goes back to status quo. This female is battered and damaged; she moves around with low self-esteem and succumbs to the whims of the treacherous. She says yes and commits even when the odds are not fair or in her favor. The Garbage Bag is non-nurturing to her man and her children, and in most cases, she is cold. She is not what you will describe as heartless, but often she lacks the real will to try. This could in part, be because she feels she has tried and failed so many times.

If this woman is the nagging type, she could break the strongest man, and tear up the home. The Garbage Bag suffers the hard consequences of her choices; mostly they are bad relationship decisions she has made that come back to haunt her like the monsters of Frankenstein. The Garbage Bag is the woman who has lost herself and constantly she makes more bad decisions. These decisions reinforce the initial choices she has made and circumstances that she has gotten herself into which shape her behaviors. The

Garbage Bag has internal scars; she is very much wounded on the inside. She might rope you down with her strings of bad blood. Unless you are Florence Nightingale, you might want to stay away from her. One of Robert Greene's 48 laws of power advises that, though the problems of The Garbage bag comes as a result of bad choices, she did not make those with the knowledge of the aftermath. She feels she has been stricken with a cascade of bad luck. She may even feel bewitched if she believes in such things. The Garbage Bag hardly looks inward for the solution to her problems; she only pushes blames on external factors. If you get involved with The Garbage Bag, my advice is to flee if you feel as if you cannot stomach her constant cycles of pain and depression.

Fleeing from her will only wound her more and push her farther away from herself.

Like all women who have mastered deception, she comes to you with a bright-outlook, with the hope that you will be the solution to all her problems. As time goes by she will begin to ask for too much, much more than reason could offer, then she will begin to alienate herself. She will regress into her old self and she leaves her man no option but to move on. Her situation is helpless and pathetic she doesn't mean to hurt anyone, yet she remains hurt herself. The Garbage Bag longs to be healed, from the inside through love and affection, but each step she takes in the direction of love, only brings her further pain. There are subtle signs to watch out for. In the initial stages before you get committed with The Garbage Bag, she is generally clingy and in need a lot of attention. She always wants to keep you engaged and be around you. The Garbage Bag will complain about the little attention she gets, while she gave none. She believes sex is the panacea to all relationship problems, until it fails. Then she withdraws and puts her eyes on the outside seeking unending gratifications. The Garbage Bag is in no way a happy woman she is always flirting with ideas of eternal happiness coming from her man, or from her job. She clings to the idea until it fails her. She could also be the career woman who will give anything for her job, or her man, but she cuts out every other thing and asphyxiates happiness out of that which she holds. The Garbage Bag is that old woman who, after a long futile chase in life remains left with nothing but a broken heart and broken dreams. She is the architect of her own misfortune, by her own hand she shoots herself in the foot constantly. When she is lucky enough to keep a man, she smolders happiness out of him as well, she infects him with her constant nagging. She in prone to cheating, due to the fact that one person cannot satisfy the vast emptiness that lies deep down within. Stay clear of her, unless you share her bleak realities. In very rare cases, The Garbage Bag finds a "perfect" man, who relishes her uncommon nature.

The Garbage Bag is one of the most vulnerable of all the women discussed in this book. She is in constant pain and she jumps at the least sign of comfort. According to Dr. Leary, the Director of the Social Psychology Program at Duke University, "...when a person's feeling is hurt by any kind of rejection, the part of the brain that processes that is the same as that which processes physical pain.

POSSIBLE SOLUTIONS

The discussion has been lengthy; we have looked at the different characteristics of the different types of Female Baggage. Of course being feminine is a common trait here, and it cuts across board. We have raised our consciousness about the different types of problems associated with the different types of baggage. Therefore, it is most appropriate to look at the possible solutions the problems raised. The possible solutions are discussed one piece of baggage at a time, in the same order by which the problems were looked at. The solutions could be related, but each one is unique and there is no one-solution cure all.

DISCLAIMER

I, the author of the content in Female Baggage can assure you, the reader, that any of the opinions expressed here are my own and are a result of the way in which my mind interprets a particular situation and/or concepts. I would like to expressly convey to you if I accidentally defame, purge, humiliate and or hurt someone's personal feelings as a result of reading and /or acting upon any or all of the information found here in this book, it is entirely unintentional.

ABOUT THE AUTHOR

It is thorough my life's experiences and through my human connection that I have learned who I am, how to love, and how to give. My very important goal is to teach others to be a better partner in their primary love relationship. Some couples disagree over personality traits or basic gender differences. Many relationships end due to misunderstandings and the buildup of anger and resentment. Although my point of view is unconcealed and matter of fact, I simply want to bring the reality of these Bags to light so you can diffuse negative feelings and aid all in love, life, and living.

Quinton Morgan

www.ingramcontent.com/pod-product-compliance
Lightning Source LLC
Chambersburg PA
CBHW060418050426
42449CB00009B/2017